T0025047

Collecting and Trading in Pokémon GO

By Josh Gregory

CHERRY LAKE PRESS

Published in the United States of America by Cherry Lake Publishing Group
Ann Arbor, Michigan
www.cherrylakepublishing.com

Reading Adviser: Marla Conn MS, Ed., Literacy specialist, Read-Ability, Inc.
Photo Credits: ©Ivan_Sabo, cover; ©amirraizat/Shutterstock, 4; ©leungchopan/Shutterstock, 6; ©F. J. CARNEROS/Shutterstock, 12;
©Stoyan Yotov/Shutterstock, 18; ©Taweepat/Shutterstock, 10, 14, 16, 20

Cherry Lake Press is an imprint of Cherry Lake Publishing Group

Library of Congress Cataloging-in-Publication Data has been filed and is available at catalog.loc.gov

Cherry Lake Publishing Group would like to acknowledge the work of the Partnership for 21st Century Learning, a Network
of Battelle for Kids. Please visit http://www.batelleforkids.org/networks/p21 for more information.

Printed in the United States of America
Corporate Graphics

Table of Contents

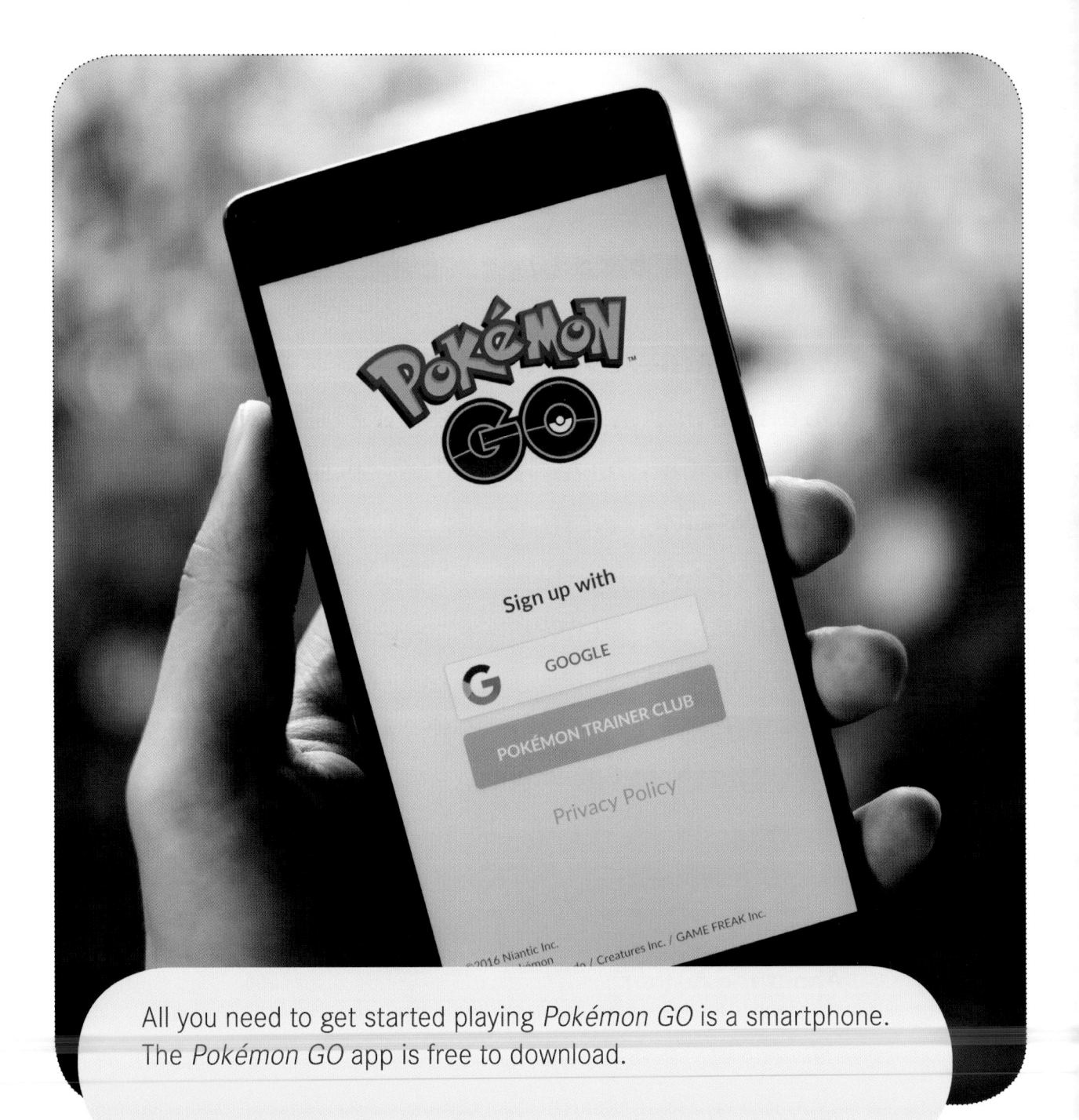

All you need to get started playing *Pokémon GO* is a smartphone. The *Pokémon GO* app is free to download.

Wild World

Every day, millions of *Pokémon GO* players grab their phones and head outside to wander their hometowns. They roam around in search of the colorful creatures known as Pokémon. One of the main goals in *Pokémon GO* is to catch every Pokémon in the game. It's not easy to do. There are hundreds of different Pokémon to find!

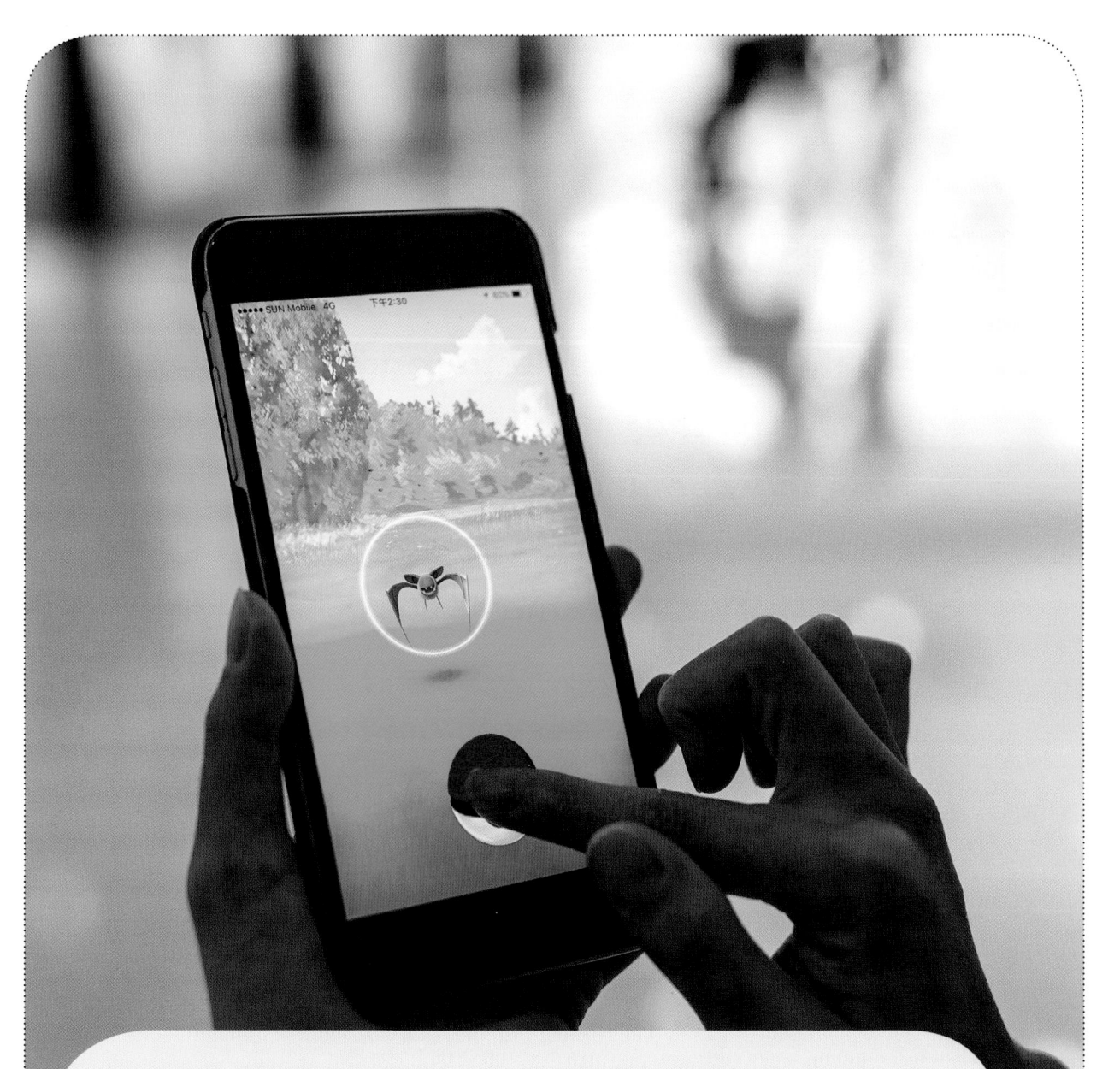

It is worth catching every Pokémon you find. Sometimes you might catch duplicates of ones you already have. This is still useful. You'll get a bunch of useful items every time you catch a Pokémon.

On the Hunt

Try walking around in different places while *Pokémon GO* is open on your phone. You'll soon notice Pokémon appearing near your character. Tap on each one you see. You'll get a close-up view of the Pokémon. Simply use your finger to swipe a Poké Ball from the bottom of the screen toward the creature.

Successful Swipes

Time your swipe carefully when you throw a Poké Ball. You want to throw the ball when the colored circle around the Pokémon is small. Make sure you aim the ball toward the middle of the circle!

POKÉDEX

CAUGHT: 59 SEEN: 84

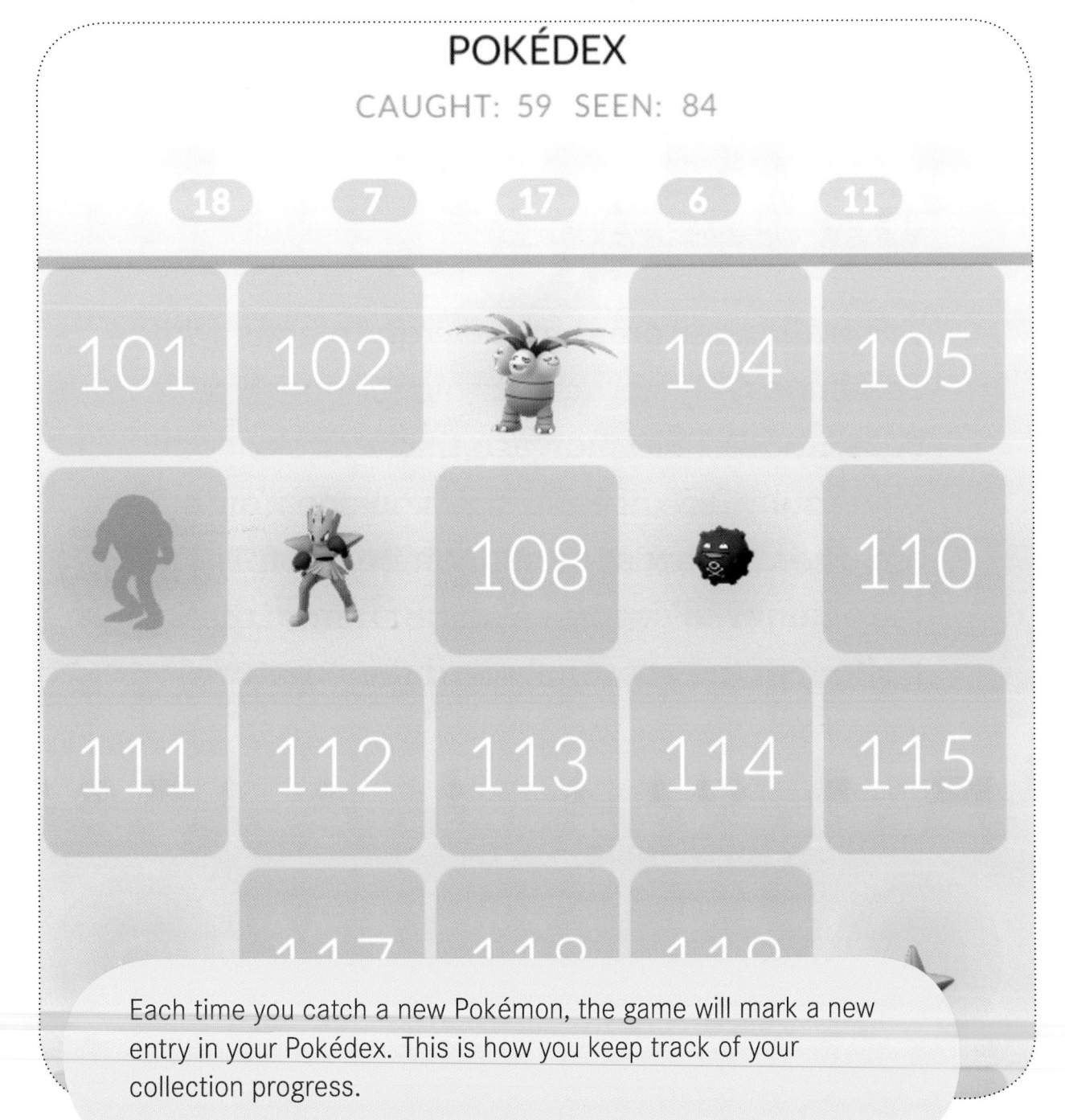

| 18 | 7 | 17 | 6 | 11 |

101	102		104	105
		108		110
111	112	113	114	115

Each time you catch a new Pokémon, the game will mark a new entry in your Pokédex. This is how you keep track of your collection progress.

Don't Let Them Get Away

Pokémon are sometimes tough to catch. You can improve your odds by feeding them Razz Berries. You can also find more powerful kinds of Poké Balls. These items are often rewards for completing goals in *Pokémon GO*. You can also get items by visiting PokéStops. PokéStops are located near real-world landmarks. Tap on each one you see. Then use your finger to spin the photo that pops up. You'll get a bunch of items!

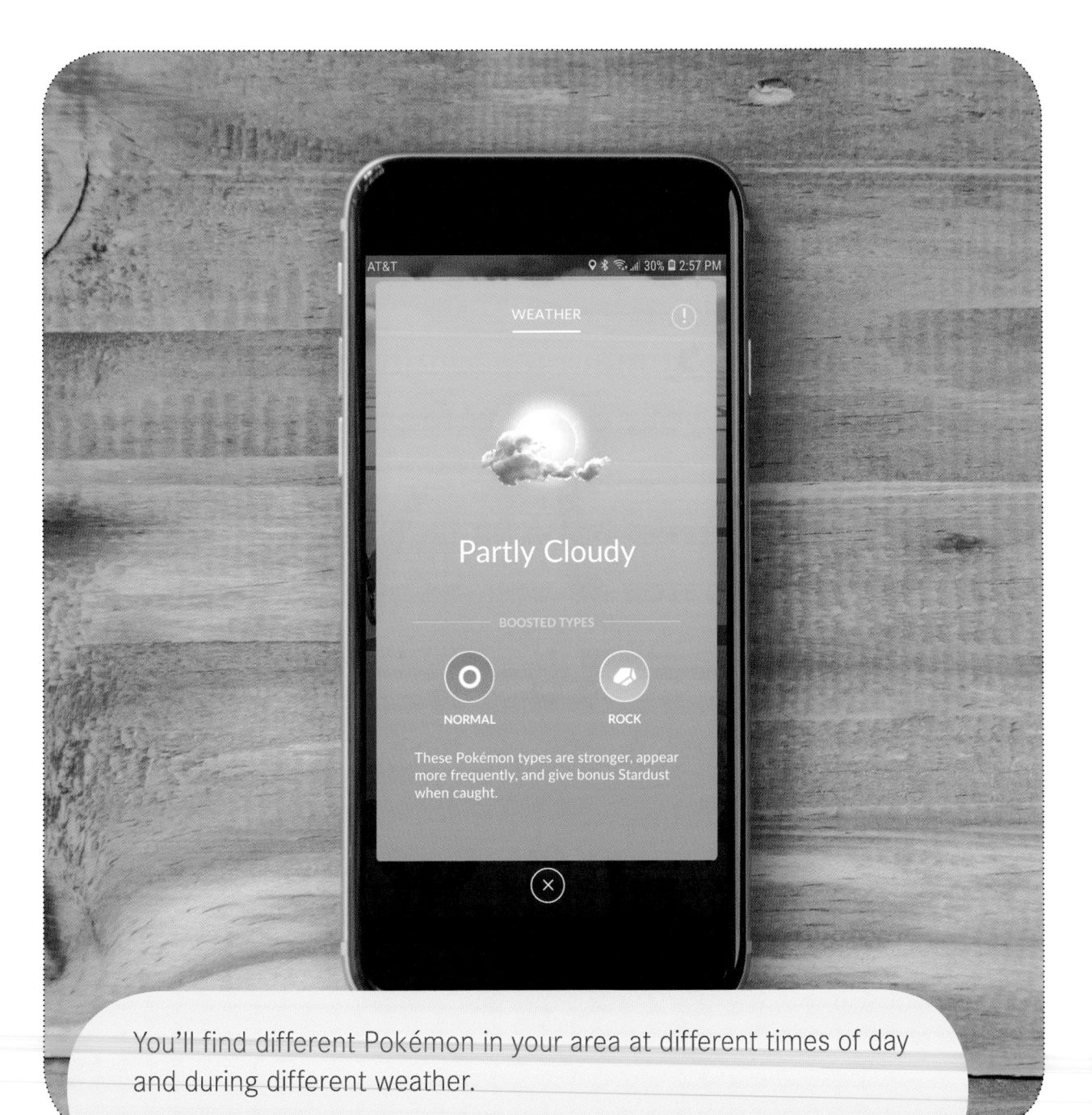

You'll find different Pokémon in your area at different times of day and during different weather.

Local Pokémon

Some Pokémon will be very easy to find. You might not even have to leave your house to catch them. Try tapping the rectangle in the bottom right corner of the screen. You will see a list of the Pokémon in your area. Choose one and tap it. Then tap the footprints that pop up. The game will show you exactly where to go to find the Pokémon.

The biggest *Pokémon GO* events can draw tens of thousands of fans to cities around the world.

Rare Finds

Not all Pokémon can be easily found in the wild. Some are **regional**. They can only be found in certain parts of the world. Legendary Pokémon can also be tough to track down. Most Legendaries can only be captured after winning tough challenges called Raid Battles. But they are some of the rarest and strongest Pokémon in the game. It's worth it to catch them!

Special Events

The **developers** of *Pokémon GO* often host special events that make it easier to catch certain rare Pokémon. Some are in-person events where players gather in one location. Others are limited-time online events.

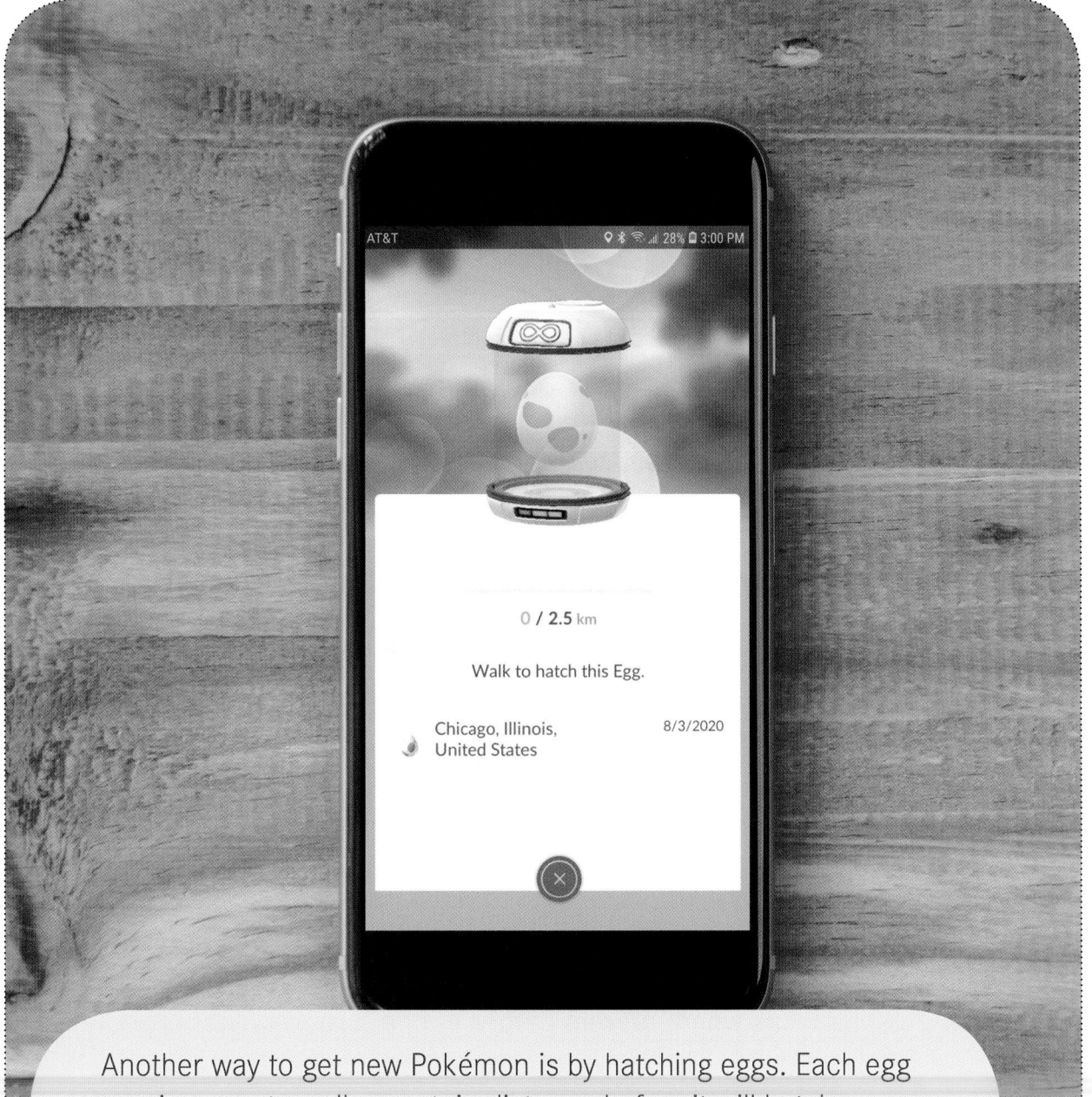

Another way to get new Pokémon is by hatching eggs. Each egg requires you to walk a certain distance before it will hatch.

One Thing Leads to Another

There are other ways to get new Pokémon besides catching them. For example, some **species** can **evolve** into new ones. To evolve a Pokémon, you need to feed it candy. Each Pokémon species has its own type of candy. You can get more candy by catching duplicate Pokémon of the same species. It sometimes takes a huge amount of candy to evolve a Pokémon!

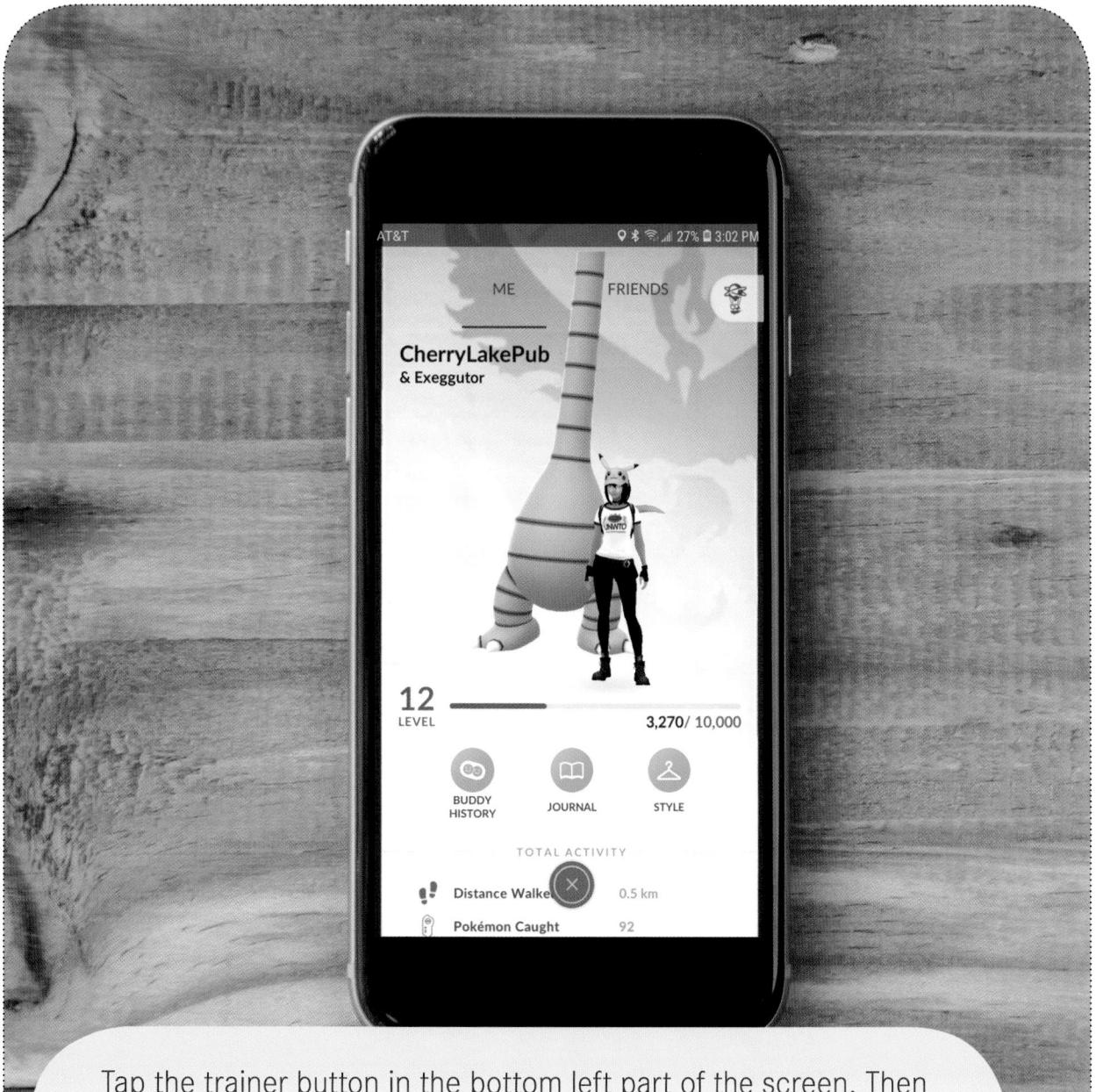

Tap the trainer button in the bottom left part of the screen. Then tap "Friends" at the top of the screen to access the Friends menu.

Making Friends

Pokémon GO is a social game. Playing with friends is a big part of the fun. Want to add another player to your in-game Friends list? First, either you or your friend will need the other person's Trainer Code. You can find your Trainer Code in the Friends menu. One player must enter the other's code in the Friends menu. Then the other person has to accept the offer. Then you will be on each other's Friends lists.

The easiest way to trade in *Pokémon GO* is in person. Ask a parent to bring you where other players are gathering to trade and battle.

Time to Trade

Your Friendship Level will increase as you battle alongside or against friends. Once you become Good Friends with someone, you will be able to trade Pokémon with them. This is a great way to fill your Pokédex! Each trade costs Stardust. You get Stardust by catching Pokémon and completing other goals.

The Power of Friendship

Increasing your friendship levels will decrease the Stardust cost of trades. Also, some rare Pokémon can only be traded between players with very high friendship levels. This means you can't get a super powerful Pokémon from someone you just met.

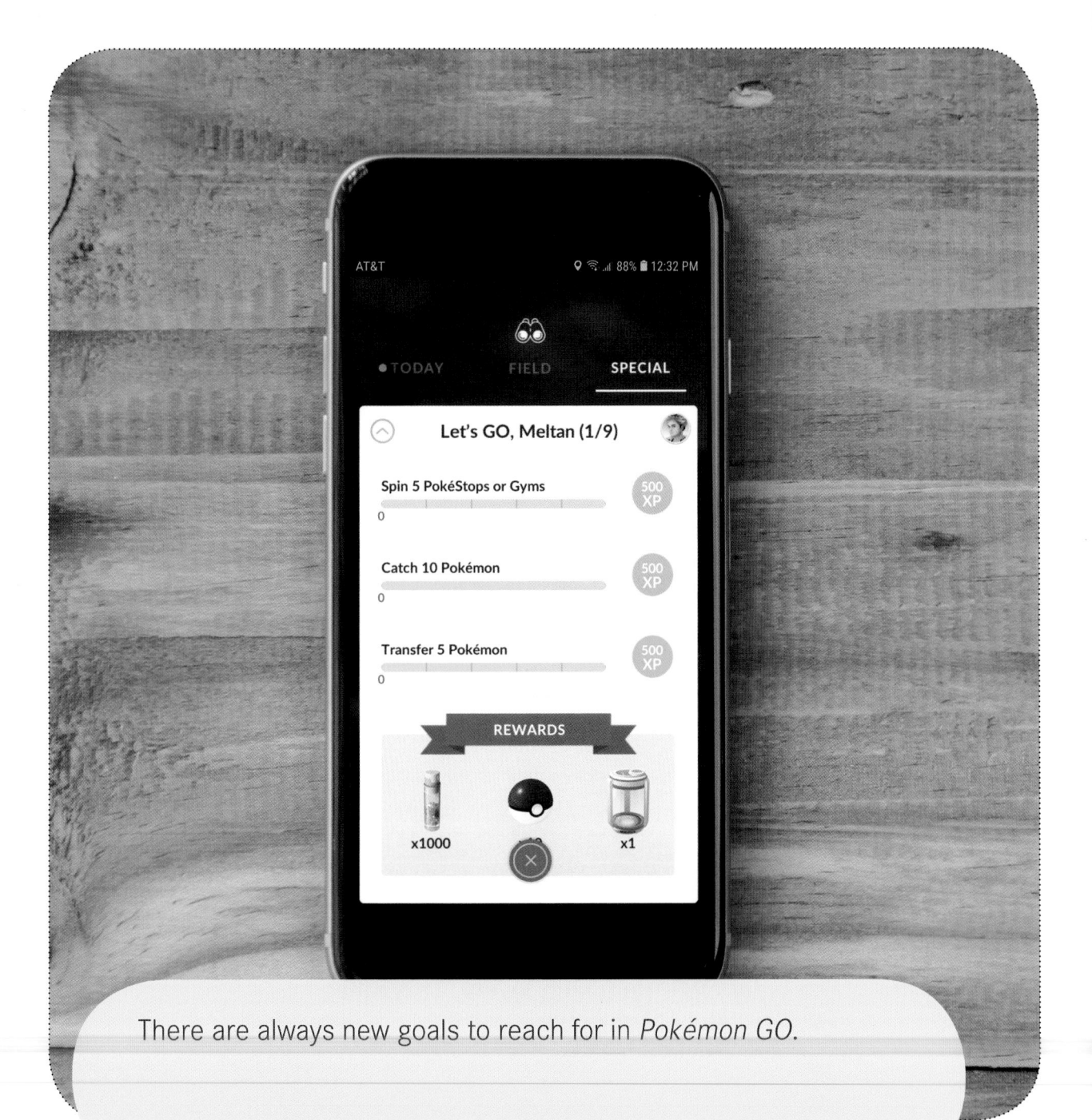

There are always new goals to reach for in *Pokémon GO*.

Completing Your Collection

Worried that you might be running out of new Pokémon to catch? Don't be. The developers are always adding new creatures to the game. You can also try tracking down special Shiny Pokémon. Shinies are extra-rare versions of regular Pokémon. The only difference is that they have different coloring. But high-level players love to collect them! Good luck!

Glossary

developers (dih-VEL-uh-purz) people who make video games or other computer programs

evolve (ih-VOLV) to change into a new form

regional (REE-juh-nuhl) found only in a certain area

species (SPEE-sheez) a specific kind of Pokémon, such as a Pikachu or Charmander

Find Out More

Books

Cunningham, Kevin. *Video Game Designer*. Ann Arbor, MI: Cherry Lake Publishing, 2016.

Powell, Marie. *Asking Questions About Video Games*. Ann Arbor, MI: Cherry Lake Publishing, 2016.

Scholastic. *Pokémon Super Deluxe Essential Handbook: The Need-to-Know Stats and Facts on Over 800 Characters*. New York: Scholastic, 2018.

Web Sites
Pokémon GO
www.pokemongo.com/en-us
Check out the official *Pokémon GO* homepage for the latest updates on what is going on in the game.

Pokémon GO Events
https://pokemongolive.com/en/events
Check the schedule to see when and where official live *Pokémon GO* events are happening.

Index

About the Author

Josh Gregory is the author of more than 150 books for kids. He has written about everything from animals to technology to history. A graduate of the University of Missouri–Columbia, he currently lives in Chicago, Illinois.